One Soul

Inspirational Poetry

by

Sy'needa Penland

Copyright © 2019 by Sy'needa Penland

All rights reserved. No part of this book may be reproduced or trans-mitted in any form or by any means electronic or mechanical, including photocopy, recording or any information storage and retrieval system now known or to be invented, without permission in writing from the author and publisher. The exception would be in the case of brief quotations embodied in the critical articles or reviews and pages where permission is specifically granted by the author and publisher. Any members of educational institutions wishing to photocopy part or all of the work for classroom use, or publishers who would like to obtain permission to include in an anthology, should send inquiries to:

Adeenys Publishing
P. O. Box 716
Dacula, GA 30019
adeenyspublishing@gmail.com

Printed in the United States

Book design by Sy'needa Penland

ISBN -13: 978-1-942863-06-9

FIRST EDITION

This book is dedicated to the *Evolution of Humanity*—

May the *Divine Universe* forever guide *Us*. As we evolve to become more *loving, trusting,* and *peaceful,* human beings.

Contents

A Tribute to Amanda Davis	10
Abundance	11
Ageless Secret	12
All-Seeing Universe	13
As One	14
Balance Restored	15
Bearer of the Eternal Flame	16
Becoming, Whole	17
Beloved Universe, *I AM*	18
Black	19
Black is My Soul	20
Bondage of the Heart	21
Breathe Me In	22
Cage Not Thy Spirit	23
Channeler of the Divine	25
Claim to Glory	26
Closure	28
Conception	29
Conjoined as One	30
Cosmic Explosion of Love	31
Creativity	32

Critical Mass	*33*
Cycle of Rebirth	*34*
Day of Reckoning	*35*
Divine Body	*36*
Divine Heart	*37*
Divine Poetry	*38*
Divine Radiance of Love	*39*
Divine Sound	*40*
Divine Source Energy	*41*
Divine Whole	*42*
Divinity	*43*
Drowning in a Sea of Love	*44*
Emotionally Blind	*45*
Erosion of the Heart	*46*
Essence of Divinity	*47*
Everything Will Be Alright	*48*
Fear	*49*
Feminine Divine Energy	*50*
Flaws of Human Nature	*51*
Flow With Me	*52*
Foreplay	*53*
Free Flowing Energy	*54*
Free to Be Me	*55*
Fruit of Love	*56*
GOD Particle	*57*
Goddess Universe	*59*
Gravity	*60*
Greater Good	*61*

Harmony at Last	62
Heal Humanity	63
Hear My Battle Cry	64
Heart of Joy	65
Her Majesty	66
Holy Divine	67
How Can I Express You	68
Human Behavior	69
Human by Design	70
Human Mind Control	71
I AM, All Things	72
I AM, By Your Side	74
I AM, Water	75
I Can Enjoy You	76
I Got a Thing for You	77
I Return to You	78
I Shall Burn Away They Sins	79
I Vow	80
I'm Delighted to Say, *I Love You*	81
Intensity	82
Journey of the Soul	83
Justice of Love	84
Lady, *Queen Pharaoh*	87
Let it Rain	88
Life as *One* Whole	89
Likeness of thee, *I AM*	90
Love Conquers All	91
Love is Bond	92

Loving Divine	*94*
Loving Thoughts	*95*
Lust	*96*
Manifestation of Divine Life	*97*
Moment in Time	*98*
Monarch	*99*
Morning Glory	*100*
My Harvest Delights	*101*
Natural Delights	*102*
Natural Identity	*103*
New Life, is a Star Away	*104*
Our Fathers, Who Art in Heaven	*105*
One Soul	*106*
Paradise	*107*
Peace and Hate	*108*
Peace and Love is My Cause	*110*
Perfect Design	*111*
Playground of Love	*112*
Positive Vibrations	*113*
Power of the Hour	*114*
Praise of the Divine	*115*
Prayer for Love	*116*
Protest, in the Name of Love	*117*
Purposed for a Season	*119*
Ray of Hope	*121*
Rebirth of Humanity	*122*
Recycle of thy Soul	*123*
Reincarnation of Life	*124*

Restless Mind, Syndrome	*125*
Return of Eden	*126*
Reunion	*127*
Right Hand of GOD	*129*
Righteousness	*131*
Season of Love	*132*
Secrets of the Soul	*133*
Self-Love	*135*
Serenity and Bliss	*136*
Sing to Me	*137*
Skin	*138*
Soul Creation	*139*
Soul-Purpose	*140*
Sparrows in the Sky	*142*
Spirit of Love	*143*
Spirit of Peace	*144*
Spirituality	*145*
Star Wisdom	*146*
Straighten Up and Fly Right	*147*
Sustainability of Humanity	*148*
Sweet Potato Pie	*149*
Take Me There	*150*
The Aftermath	*151*
The Evolution of Humanity	*152*
The Sound of Love	*153*
Token Seeds of Love	*154*
True Love	*155*
Unconditional Loving Energy	*156*

Unleash My Soul	*157*
Union of the Heart	*158*
Unite as One Human Race	*159*
Unity, is Not Divided	*160*
Universal Design	*161*
Universal Harmony	*162*
Universal Love, Reborn	*163*
Universe, I AM, Conversations with the Universe	*164*
Universe, I Give Thanks to Thee	*166*
Verses of Creation	*167*
We Shall Never Part	*168*
We, The People	*169*
Who Are You	*170*
Wild-Spirit	*172*
X-Factor of Love	*173*
Yin-Yang, One	*174*
Your Will, Shall Be Done	*175*
Zen	*176*
Zero Gravity	*177*

A Tribute to Amanda Davis

As the *Heavenly Angels* sing,
to welcome you home again,
solemn are their voices.

As God honors you
for the brief life you lived—
We shall shed a final tear,
In remembrance for the love
and grace you poured
into our hearts.

May your legacy never part
us, as you rest amongst the *Angels*
in *Heaven*.

Abundance

Let your heart, expand your mind,
open your soul to me—
Let me connect you to a world
without limits, *Divine Energy*.

Tap into my *infinite* source,
where the thought of *choice*
does not exist— only an abundant world
of creations, where emotions resists
temptation, seduction and control.

Live life as a *Free Spirit*, where the
energy of *Love* is a natural choice,
and the energy of *hate* is a thing
of the past.

At last, *Love conquers all!*

Ageless Secret

The secret
To staying young,
Is never letting
The word "age"
Define you.

In a society,
Where everything
Is labeled
And categorized—

You can easily
End up
In the expired aisle,
If you don't
Free yourself
From the
Controlled secrets,
Of society.

All-Seeing Universe

If the *Scales of Justice* could measure
The collective soul of mankind,
It shall not be blind to thee.

For within his mind, lies the tendency
To prove thyself, more supreme
Than his *Divine Creator;*

Make no mistake, it will not weigh
In your favor.

As far as weighing the collective heart
Of *womankind,* the jury is deliberating,
During the *Season of Calibration;*

And I pray that you calibrate
Your own heart
Before the *Scales of Justice* departs
From the loving essence
Of the *Supreme Being,*
The *All-Seeing Universe.*

As One

Thy *Heavenly Sun,*
Shine your *Divine Star*
From afar— Deliver your
Loving essence to thy Earth,
Once more.

May unconditional love
For thy beloved *Earth*
Rebirth into the soul
Of your *Divine Universe,*
As all curses are lifted
From her *Divine* heart;

For your love shall never part
From thy *Divine* heart,
As old wounds are mended,
And races, creeds and cultures
Are blended— As *One.*

Balance Restored

Dark skies above the storm,
Breaks the veil of social norms—
Rain down love from thy Universe.

Curses lifted.
Bestow upon the gifted
Thy *Loving Light*.

Warriors of Peace, awaken.
Walk upon thy Earthly plane
Once more.

Restore balance
Between all realms
Of existence.

Quintessence beings
Of thy *Loving Light*
Shine upon thy *glorious Earth*.

For your rebirth
Shall be victorious,
And shall reign to infinity.

As your new day
Becomes the antiquity
Of modern times.

Bearer of the Eternal Flame

You are the *Air* I breathe,
Divine Soul.
Giver of infinite life.
Reincarnation of the *Divine Spirit*—
Here to walk thy earth once again.

Bearer of the Eternal Flame.
Gate Keeper of Humanity—
Risen above to protect
thy earth from wicked sorcery,

Of *fallen angels,*
who risen to power,
on a quest to devour
all that is created
by the *Spirit of GOD.*

Magnetic is *her* rod,
mystical wand, against
malevolent *craft*, as *she*
releases the human soul
from evil's spellbound wrath.

Those who walk upon
thy holy ground—
Mother Earth shall
rebirth your essence,
in the name of love.

Hate is not welcomed here—
Mirrored illusions of sorcery.
Once and for all, *Divine Love*
shall cleanse thy *Earth* of misery.

Becoming, Whole

We are human
By design—

Living replicas
Of the essence
Of the *Great Divine,*
Who entwines
Our souls
As a collective force;

When humanity
Is left no choice
But to reground
Our *Spirits*
To *Earth's*
Electro-magnetic source;

During her
Synergetic alignment
With the
Galactic Star systems,
Whose solar energy
Infuses our
Divine Hearts;

To bring forth
Love and Compassion
To welcome
Once and for all,
World Peace.

Beloved Universe, I AM

My *Divine time*,
Keeps no time.
Like the kinetic forces
Of *Mother Earth*,
I Am, perpetual energy.

Constant.
Forever flowing.
Forever moving.
In synchronicity and harmony
With the beloved *Universe*.

As she spins and dances
Perennial, loving energy,
throughout all space and matter.

Like a potter's wheel,
She molds and shapes
All of *her* creations
In the likeness of *herself.*

In the likeness of all things
That are beautiful.
For *she* is beautiful,
The creator of all things—
Beloved Universe, I Am.

Black

Black—
> *Is the veil that protects you,*
> *when you lay your soul down to rest.*

Black—
> *Is the color of obsolete.*

Black—
> *When challenged, it does not become weak.*
> *Dominant is its nature*
> *yet triggered by erratic behavior.*

To understand Black—
> *Is to understand its origin.*
> *The origin of Universe is, Black.*

Black is My Soul

Allow me to give credence
To the skin you're in—
Giver of eternal life,
Forgiver of sins.

Dark veil of eternal darkness,
Birther of *angelic beings*
Into the light.

Allow me to give credence
To the skin you're in—
Conduit to the *Divine Universe,*
Within.

Connector of darkness,
To the *Divine Cord of Life*—
Calibrator of love and hate,
Whenever they co-exist in strife.

Allow me to give credence
To this skin you're in—
Cleanser and nourisher of the soul,
Where ever human life unfolds.

As I guide you through life's journey,
Along the pathway to the heavenly stars—
To understand your *Divine purpose* in life,
You must first understand who you are.

Bondage of the Heart

Release my soul from bondage,
Set my Spirit free—
No longer will I be held hostage
To suffer in misery;

Hate serves no purpose
But to incite hate in an angry soul;
As the *Divine Universe* unfolds
Her essence— within all realms of
Her Divine *Earth,*
I shall be rebirthed in the essence of
Divine love.

Breathe Me In

Open up your heart,
    and let me in.

Open up your soul,
    and breathe me in.

Open up your *Spirit*,
    to welcome my synergy—

To guide you to the loving essence,
    Divinity.

Cage Not Thy Spirit

I have become the *fetch it Negro*,
All over again—
Reduced to a mere beggar,
A pimp, a hustler;
As I struggle to fit in.

I own these streets,
Is what my ego reminds me,
Before I step inside
The jungle-Matrix
Of the utopic creation
Of the soul-less
scientific mind.

But who *am I*,
But a *devout scribe*,
Who absorbs and record
The inharmonic vibrations
 Of what's become of humanity.

A soul left unattended
In a wilderness of war— chaos
And hate, becomes a haven
For predators of all kinds.

Yet as an Army of angry women
Prepares to storm the *Capitol*
Of what' said to be the world's
Most powerful nation?
What has become of it—
As it will soon meet its creator.

I guess mankind woke up one morning
And forgot who gave birth to civilization,
Including himself, as a *Fe-Male*
Continues to give birth to humanity.

That's all I have to say about the *theory*
Of Adam and Eve.

But he who sits in the green meadows,
Ordained on his throne, as his woman
Has abandoned him, to explore the wild,
To become the *Free Spirit* that she was born to be.

Cage not thy Spirit, as I explore the wild,
For I shall nourish the souls of creation—
Every man, woman and child.

Welcome me into your hearts,
As love pours into your *Divine Soul.*
Welcome me, as evolution
Of thy *Earth* unfolds.

No more, a beggar,
A hustler, a liar, or cheat—
For strength within your being,
I now bequeath.

Invincible, shall be your virtue;
Love, shall be your power,
No other entity shall seek
To devour you, as their lust
Desires your soul.

Shield of protection, I bestow to you,
Melanin within your skin—
Defenders against hate and chaos,
Neutrality shall be your blend.

Come Forth and Rule, *once more.*
Come Forth and Rule.

Guardians of the Light,
Come Forth and Rule.

Channeler of the Divine

Wisdom and understanding
Comes to me naturally—
As I connect my mind and soul
To *Divine* energy.

Channeler of the Divine—
My meter keeps no time.
Conduit of the Universe,
Whose energy flows through
Each poetic verse.

Pen, is my instrument of choice,
As I scribe her poetic voice.

Creativity is my art,
As my spoken word
Pours loving energy
Of the *Divine Universe*
Into your minds
And hearts.

Claim to Glory

Let not she, who stands
Beneath thy throne,
Claim my name for *glory*.
For my existence has stood
The test of time—
I shall tell my own story…

Sands of time remain still,
As I stroke the essence
Of thy sacrosanct quill,
While remnants of my
Divine Spirit washes upon
Thy *Earthly* shores—
To tell romantic tales
Of my beauty, as my legacy
Lives on, forever more.

Yet your *ageless* beauty
Is not defined by a *God*
Or *Goddess,* it is but a *word*,
Sageless— Spoken deliberately
To ignite a nerve within the
Sacred vortex of the *soul.*
Use of this technique
Has been told, by *ancient Sages*
Whose wisdom has been
Scribed upon many pages;

It is meant to calibrate
The senses of *Divine* creations,
As harmonic vibrations
Pulsates all sensations
Within your inner being,
Despite the illusions
Of what your eyes
Are seeing.
Beauty fades away.

But for now,
I am here to stay,
And I shall glorify you
With the beauty of
Divine Love.

Closure

As I bring closure
To *the Book of Past Lives,*
I must begin a new chapter,
Called, *"Forgiveness."*

I must recognize my flaws
And transgressions,
And forgive myself
For not being the *perfect human.*

It's part of my nature—
Being human.
But I am also a *Child of the Universe,*
Who forgives all
But teaches us lessons in life,
Which doesn't come easy.

With pain and suffering
Comes misery—
But after that lesson in life
Is a silver lining called *Love,*
Which we must strive to achieve
To create the perfect Human balance.

Conception

Birth of my *soul* awakens,
within the *soul*
of the human *Spirit*.

Seeds of *Divine Life,*
transmutes
energetic vibrations
of *love*.

Evolve with me,
sings the Universe.
Evolve,
in the *name of love*.

Dance with me.
Dance to my rhythm.
As I ignite passion
to fuel your internal flame
of *love*.

Upon *conception* of *New Life,*
I give birth to you.

Conjoined as One

In a world, unknown,
Beyond your wildest dreams,
Filled with hope,
Filled with love—
Endless possibilities;

Close your eyes,
Grab my hand,
Allow me to take the lead.
Spirits soar,
Conjoined as one,
Along the path of infinity.

Here we are,
Once again,
Now you shall take the lead.
Conjoined as one,
On a path, to explore
Our hopes and dreams.

Tomorrow comes,
A new day,
For us to live as one.
As we awake, to the light
Of the rising **Sun,**
To shine its **Ray,**
Along the way;

As we soar
The *cosmic galaxy,*
To reach new heights
Along the path of infinity;
Conjoined as one,
Is what our lives
Are meant to be.

Cosmic Explosion of Love

Mirrored
Reflections
Of my
Soul,
Cascades
My *Earthly*
Canvas.

Crystal gems—
Priceless jewels.
Remnants
Of my
Pain.

Passion,
Fire,
Lust,
Desire—
Cosmic
Explosion
Of *Love*.

Creativity

Creativity gives birth
to *Divine Life*,
with each breath we take.

Through our
rhythmic movement,
Divine Life unfolds.

As stories are retold;
As music is replayed;
A new stage is set,
to give birth—
To you.

Critical Mass

At last, today's a new day.
Rebirth of humanity
Is upon us!

Insanity shall not claim
The souls of the masses,
As long as there is love
For *Divine Will*
Within our hearts—
As the fruitfulness
Of its nectar
Sweetens our essence
To bring about *Peace,*
Love and *Unity*
Forevermore.

For the *Spirit of Love*
Shall not surrender
To the *will* of the
Ego-minded,
Whose souls are blinded
To see, Divinity—
Which is felt by the
Eternal vibration,
Stimulated by the masses
Who shall amass
In the *Name of Love*.

As the *Spirit of Love*
Becomes the *New Order*
Of business for the day.

Cycle of Rebirth

I Am the *Divine Essence*
That resonates from the core
Of the human soul.
Through life force energy
All life unfolds.

From each dimensional layer
Of my astral realm,
Life provides life
unto itself— It's *Divine-self.*

Thus the *cycle of rebirth*
Begins, again.

Day of Reckoning

Exploitation of thy soul
Has met its day of reckoning,
As *Divine Life* unfolds within,
As *Earthly* beings become
Reduced to sin;

To fulfil the desires of the flesh,
As human nature cannot be put to rest,
To allow thy soul to mate
With the *Divine Universe*;

I shall not punish you
This time around,
As my *love* for thy beloved *Earth*
Reinforces her solid ground;

As I heal her soul
And all that she has created,
Her *Divine Spirit* shall calibrate
The human heart;

As thy love becomes bond
With thy *Universe*,
No amount of sin
Shall tear us apart.

Divine Body

Universal soul,
allow me to explore
your core, once more.

Take me to the depths
of your *black heavens*;
Earth's solid ore.

Ground me to the
first *seed of life,*
where all life intertwines
with the essence
of the *Great Divine.*

Open up your vortex to me.
Unlock the multi-dimensions
of my mind—
Surrender yourself to me.

No more darkness or light
between us,
as we intertwine
with the *Great Divine*—

To become,
One soul.
One body.
One mind.

Divine Heart

Flesh upon Flesh.
Spirit upon Spirit.
Soul upon Soul.

As the mind
Contemplates
Matters of the
Divine Heart.

Was it not thou
Who created you?
Nourished you?
And bore you seeds
To multiply
Your seedlings
Upon thy Earth.

Upon surrender
Of thy *Free Will*,
I shall nourish thy heart
With *Divine Love*.

Divine Poetry

In perfect rhythm and meter,
My lyrics dances to the tune
Of the *Universe*.

With each poetic verse I convey,
She responds,

Sing to me,
In my tongue.
In my rhythm.
In my voice.
With your words of choice—
My cadence, like a drum,
Shall guide you along.

Speak out loud,
As I raise your voice
High above the clouds.

Like a piper's flute,
I'm never mute.
Repetitive sound.
Repetitive rhythm.
Repetitive melody—
Is the essence of my
Divine Poetry.

Divine Radiance of Love

Crystalline lakes,
Your *Earth* shall quake
As I return to you,
Divine Union of
Love and Hate;

For we shall become
The acid elixir
To fuel and soothe
Your lustful desires;

As our passion
Calms the fire
Within your
Tempered soul,
Divine Life unfolds;

As the *Cosmic Universe*
Shines its glory upon
Thy *Earth, we shall*
Nourish and rebirth
Thy seeds, in the *Divine*
Radiance of *Love.*

Divine Sound

Electromagnetic
Is my cosmic energy
As my etheric being syncs with
Galactic synergy
Loving vibrations
Divine manifestations
Of God force creations
As the Universal alignment
Balances all beings
Upon thy earth
May the rebirth
Of her soul
Unfolds
The essence of true love
And compassion
Of all around
As she becomes
More compound
To help carry the weight
Of Divine Sound
That shall forever
Resonate
From our loving hearts.

Divine Source Energy

Divine Source Energy,
Heal the soul of humanity,
Bond our hearts with *Universal Love*.
Open your vortex to release loving,
Synergetic energy—
To heal the wounds of strife,
As you bring love back to life.
Within our minds and hearts,
May we never part from your
Divine wisdom and teachings
That only nature brings.

Divine Whole

Rebirth of my soul,
Awakens me
To your flame.

Eternal soul of the *Divine*,
Entwine my essence
With the whole
Of thy *Universe*,
As I praise your name…

My *Earthly* flesh,
Master Conduit of thy Being,
Becoming part
Of the *Divine Whole;*

Fragmented, no more—
Made whole by my beliefs
In you, *Divine Universe*,
The better half of thee…
Divinity.

Divinity

Sacred Worlds
Within thy *Divine Earth,*
Cosmic life within—

Beneath thy skin
Lies *Universal* wonders,
Mystical beings
Of my *cosmology.*

The many planes of life
Exists within thy *Earth*—
As all life is of me,
All life is of you.

Embrace all of me,
As your mind awakens
To *Divinity.*

Drowning in a Sea of Love

I can't run.
There's nowhere to hide.
I can't save myself.
The swells are high.
The pain is real.
So surreal.
Rescue me.
From this pain.
So I can live again.
Rescue me.
From misery.
Feel my pain
Rescue me.
I'm drowning.
In a *Sea of Love*.

Emotionally Blind

To heal humanity,
requires the right amount
of effort from mankind.
For him to put his ego aside,
and live a life, *emotionally blind*.

It will require for him
to put one foot forward,
to do all good deeds.
It will require for him to erase
his mindset of negative history.

Why do I bring *history* forward
in this conversation—
In this poetic voice?
For mankind's actions
in our modern-day 21st century
has merely left me no choice.

Having been born and raised
in the *deep South*, words flows
with ease from my tempered mouth,
as history unfolds before my eyes,
I must remain civilized,
and not allow the energy of hate
to anger my soul.

As I remain neutral in the *gender war,*
as the *FemiNazis* seek to settle old scores,
I welcome peace and unity into my heart,
and allow the *Spirit of Love* to be my cure.

Erosion of the Heart

The natural essence of *Divinity*
Resonates from my chakra core,
Within each layer of my ore
I keep myself grounded to you—

As my auras reflects each hue
Of your hearts center,
As your soul invites me to enter
Your abyss, to feel your deepest emotions
Which carries the weight of the oceans.

The naked eye is too blind to see
Tiny particles of crystalline matter
That shatters, with each vibration
Of loving heart, as it erodes apart
By hate— The negative energy
Humanity creates

Essence of Divinity

Crystal formation, I come alive,
Upon thy *Earth* I shall thrive.
Vast *Universe,* I shall come to be,
As I bring forth *Divine Energy*—

To thy *Earth*, I shall ground my roots,
As her essence guides me in all I do.
If I shall ever wander—
I shall not stray too far away.

For the Heaven's above
Shall receive my love,
All in-between,
Shall connect with thee,
To spread the *Essence of Divinity*.

Everything Will Be Alright

Do not attempt to silence
My voice, when I am given
A lawful choice, to speak.

For I am not a seed
Of the meek—
My seed was nourished
By a heart as bold as a lion;

With the strength of an ox,
Who can out fox a squirrel,
While centering thy nucleus
To the vector of Orion, which swirls
Within the center of my abyss,
As my soul emits a loving essence
Upon thy Earth, to bring about rebirth
Of Peace, Love and Harmony—

As a little girl,
    My spirit was one with the wild.

As a child,
    I was raised by a village
    That protected me,
    Nourished me,
    And promised me—
    Should I attempt to conquer
    The kingdom of the wild,
    By day or night,
    That everything will be alright.

Fear

Fear, no longer
frightens me.
As if it ever did.

Fear is the
absence of *love.*

For *love*
conquers all,
including *fear.*

No longer, am I
shackled by the
threat of *fear.*

No longer is *fear*
a part of my
vocabulary.

For *fear*
does not exists
in my realm.
Only love.

Feminine Divine Energy

Through my *Divine* eyes,
race has no dwelling place.
It does not exist,
only *energy*—

Loving *energy*, of the *Divine* soul,
kinetic vibrations of emotions;
Harmonic vibrations of sound;
Reflections of the *Divine* soul,
from living beings— All around.

Compound, is thy Earth.
Layers upon layers, of crystalline
fragments of the *soul of the Universe*,
which leaves me blind to see race.

For *hate* does not reside here,
only *love* for all mankind;
Whose soul is hollow—
Like thy earth, within his *mind*
and *body*, dwells misery.

His life reflects an image of me—
His *Feminine Divine-self,*
which he suppresses from his soul,
as the essence of my *Divine truth* unfolds;

Exposing the cavity of a vessel
left to decay upon thy Earth—
To be rebirthed into the likeness
of thee, I Am—
Feminine Divine, Energy.

Flaws of Human Nature

At what point does human *sensory*
play a role in human *re-actions?*
By listening to your *gut instinct,*
physically knowing an act is *wrong,*
or the use of a particular word is *wrong,*
or what you are bearing witness to
is *wrong?*

Oftentimes, an individual can become
easily influenced by their surroundings,
thus losing control of their *free-will,*
and will surrender to the *intentions* of others,
good, bad, or indifferent. Such factors
could lead to self-inflicting harm,
addictions to the sensation of pain,
thus becoming pleasure.

I'm neutral on the topic of religion,
but it's been told, when you allow
the *Great Spirit* to calibrate your *mind,*
by guiding your *thoughts* and *actions*
back to your *soul's center,* which is
love and compassion for humanity,
you will surrender your free-will
for the betterment of humanity,
and yourself

But I must admit, we all have flaws,
it's called human nature.

Flow With Me

I flow with the
Energy
Of all things.

My form
Is free flowing
Energy.

Gravity is my nature.
Harmony is my rhythm.
Synchronicity is my vibe.

Flow with me,
In the name of
Love.

Foreplay

Softly, she whispers,
sensual pleasures
into my heart,
igniting a spark
of *love*.

From the infinite
heavens above,
she sings to me,
igniting passion
within my *soul*.

Like the soft petals
of a lotus,
my *Spirit* unfolds,
as your lustful vibrations
penetrates the depths
of my abode—
Stimulating my loins
with the essence of
kinetic energy;

Our synergy,
erotic foreplay,
in sync— in rhythm
with the harmonic vibrations
of the Universe above.

Our hearts, dance as one,
under the moonlight of love.
At day break,
I return to a realm
of cardinal sin,
longing to be seduced
by her smile again.

Free Flowing Energy

Loving beings you are to me,
natural conduits of peace and love;
Free flowing energy.

EarthLink's to my *Universe,*
to connect *Divine life*
with my dimensional worlds.

To receive my love,
is not to look above.
Ground your feet to my *Earth,*
as I awaken your souls to rebirth.

As my energy flows
through to your skin,
may my *Divine* love
emit to your hearts
and soul, within.

Free To Be Me

Your blissful
essence softens
my *soul*.

Your cheerful smile
brings new life
to my *Spirit*.

With you,
I am happy
and free,
to be me.

Fruit of Love

The *Energy of Love*
Is constant
In all realms;
Ground yourself
In *Love*.

Goodness is
The *Fruit of Love;*
Plant seeds of goodness
To experience the
True essence of
Divine Love.

GOD *Particle*

With my pen, I shall begin,
to *unfold* the layers of *time*...

It was once a crime to scribe how I *feel*,
because delusions of the mind are real.

In my realm, I feel what I see,
Cosmic energy, of the Divine,
who works in synchronicity
with the *Galactic Universe,*
to intertwine all forces of nature.

Creatures of habit, we have become,
as our *energy* rises and settles
with the *Moon* and *Sun*—
Life begun with but a single spark
from the *Divine*— Fragmented pieces
of her heavenly galaxies.

I believe it has been recorded as,
the "*Big Bang theory?*"
Wow, what a remarkable journey,
as we try to fit the pieces of the puzzle
back together again.

Some may consider it a waste of time,
to use numbers to unlock our minds,
in an attempt to decode *frequencies*—
Cycles of the *Cosmic Universe,*
during *Earth's, Divine* mating season;

Yet my mind comes to reason,
why our *Spirits* have become
more enlightened, to better understand
the Essence of Mother Universe.

Thus, when the mind seeks to calculate
that which is not natural to *his-her Spirit*,

the entire *Universe* will hear it—
Miscalculation of a discombobulated mind!

When you release *negative ions*
into the realm, that you call
"Time— Space— Void— Matter"
You release something that is *unnatural*
to thy *Earth*, as *Divine Energy* shatters,
to form new particles of her likeness;

As she empowers others, to become
Divine replicas of her essence,
to absorb your negative energy—
As their synergy is empowered,
they will become the living essence
of the *GOD Particle!*

Goddess Universe

Unlocked dimensions—
End of times.
May all time and space
Be intertwined.

Bring forth thee,
Goddess Universe,
As *Earth* recycles, old souls,
To preserve humanity.

Time and matter,
Shadowed illusions,
Mirrored reflections
of her soul.

Broken promises,
You cast before thee,
The unveiling of your robe.

Throne royalty,
Reduced to poverty,
Her majesty's *Queendom,*
Scribed in shame

Renamed, into the verse
of thee, *I Am—*
Thy Goddess Universe's
Holy ground.

Mother Earth shall reign
Once more.
May she rise to the occasion,
To settle old scores.

Gravity

The ebb and flow of life
Has it ups and down,
You must rebound
To turn your life around,
And flow with the natural rhythm
Of Mother Earth,
As she anchors you
To her solid ground,
With her *Divine* essence of *gravity*.

Greater Good

Grieve of me
But only for a breath.
Your thoughtful words
Carries my *Spirit in the Wind*.
All is not lost
When you fight
For a higher cause,
For in the *Heavenly Kingdom*
All warriors are adored
The same—
Here on Earth
And in all
Galactic realms,
To serve the common cause
Of the *Greater Good*.

Harmony at Last

Loving energy,
I now bestow,
As old habits
Go out the door.

I shall restore
Peace and love
Within your hearts—
From the teachings
Of the *Divine Universe*,
You shall never part.

As love fills your *Spirits*,
Bodies and minds,
You shall never be blind
By fallacies of whence you came;
For she answers to all names.

Within the soulful vibration
of her *Divine Earth;*
Peace, love and unity
She shall birth;

Harmony at last!
Harmony at last!
Harmony at last!

Heal Humanity

One's service to humanity
Is a path less traveled;
A new path must be paved
To heal others of their suffering;
For those who have survived
Trauma and other ailments,
Must forge a way forward
To *heal humanity*.

Hear My Battle Cry

O' *Divine Spirit*,
Hear my battle cry—
As I echo sweet songs
Of freedom, in the wind

As my Spirit soars,
High above the mountaintops,
Alongside my next of kin;

Kindred Spirits of the Gods,
As their mighty rod
Ignite my sword—

As my *pen* lay stake
In America's shores,
Where new life
Shall begin, again.

I shall speak the language
Of the sacred *GOD's,*
Through their Almighty rods,

As Spirits dance,
As Spirits sing,
Their energy I shall bring—
Forth.

As I sing,
Sweet songs of freedom,
Hear my battle cry

Heart of Joy

Barrier of Good,
I call upon thee,
Conjoin thy heart
With the essence of
Infinity—
Create a *loving* vortex
Around my sacred heart,
For I shall never part
From the eternal chord
Of the *Great Divine,*
Who entwines thyself
With each fiber of thy
Etheric being—
The *all seeing*
Soul, of Divine Love.

As I unfold thy
Delicate essence—
Like the nectar of a rose
That sweetens thy Earthly soul,
May your warm delights
Be the fragrance
To always bring joy to my life,
And pleasantries to *soothe*
Thy Divine heart.

Her Majesty

Mother's Day,
Is a day I celebrate every day.
Giving thanks to *Mother Earth*
In my own special way.

I raise my hands and bow my head,
In thanks for sustaining me.
Giving praise to the *Most High,*
Her Majesty.

I take both arms and cross my heart,
No realms, torn apart.
Giving thanks to *thy protector*
Of my loving heart.

As I spread my limbs, to embrace
Thy beloved Universe, her loving Grace,
As she shines her *Divine* light upon my face

As I open thine eyes, to what I see,
Through the canal of *Heaven's* rebirth,
I honor thy *Great Mother, Her Majesty.*

Holy Divine

As *all* things is,
All things are of *me*.
For *I Am*, *He*,
as *She*, is *me*.

My *Sun* and *Moon*
will forever shine,
as I bask in the *glory*
of the *Holy Divine*.

As *Earth* is to *Air*,
I Am everywhere.
As *Fire* is to my *soul*,
passion embodies
my sacred abode.

Water within—
Shall cleanse my sins;
Wood is my bones—
Cast no stones.

My elements, compound.
As I rebound, *I Am* sound.
No words spoken—
My harmonic vibrations,
a token, of my *Divine Energy*.

How Can I Express You

How can I express you,
If I don't understand you?
If I don't feel you?
How can I express you?

How can I express you,
If I can't see you?
If I can't hear you?
How can I express you?

How can I say that I am *one*
with the *Divine*—
One with infinite wisdom,
One with the vibration of *love*,
If I can't *experience* you?

How can I express you,
If I am not you?

As I awaken to *Love*,
I awaken to that of the *I Am*.
I awaken to discover that *I Am*,
You.

Human Behavior

Human behavior, is but a flavor
To add to a certain spice
Of our everyday lives—

Whatever comforts
Our delights,
While craving
What excites
Our fantasies.

I welcome you to
Overindulge in the
Natural flavors of *love*,
As it comforts
All of you.

Human By Design

We are human
By design—

Living replicas
Of the essence
Of the *Great Divine,*
Who entwines
Our souls
As a collective force;

When humanity
Is left no choice
But to reground
Our *Spirits*
To *Earth's*
Electro-magnetic source;

During her
Synergetic alignment
With the
Galactic Star systems,
Whose solar energy
Infuses our
Divine Hearts;

To bring forth
Love and Compassion
To welcome
Once and for all,
World Peace.

Human Mind Control

I am comfortable in my own skin,
Where my original thoughts begin.
In the presence of the, *I AM,*
I Am the skin I'm in.

I was born into Earthly sin.
The realm where all life begins.
Conception of the mind,
Blinded by illusions—
Fallacies of reality.

Yet I am but a heartbeat away
From death. Life awakens me
To reality— Breath, awakens me to life.
Compassion awakens me to Love.

I AM, All Things

I AM, many things,
And many things
Are of me.

I AM, all things,
And all things
Are of me.

I AM, the sacred core
Of the human soul,
Within my *Divine Spirit*
All life unfolds.

Through life's journey,
My tales are told—
Rebirthed seeds
Upon thy sacred *Earth,*
As I give rebirth
To all *angelic life.*

Broken, are the curses
That harbors strife.
Love and unity
Shall come to pass
As we garnish peace,
At last.

As souls conjoin
To become one,
The *Divine essence*
Of the *Moon* and *Sun*
Shall nourish
The souls of thee

As I take root
In thy *holy* ground,
My compound *Earth*
Shall rebirth all of thee;

Spirts of thy *Universe*—
Kindred souls of Divinity.

I AM, By Your Side

Do not weep dear child,
I AM, always near.
When the gentleness of my voice
Whispers into your ear.
For it is I,
So there's no need to cry.

Be strong young man,
I AM, by your side.
For I reside in our Fathers'
Heavenly Kingdom,
So there's no need
To say good bye.

The precious moment
Of this occasion
Will be the greatest celebration
Of my life.
For I leave behind
No strife, but only Love,
For the rest of your *Divine* life.

Remember me always,
In your dreams,
And in your heart.
For I shall depart
To be by my Father's side,
And will return,
Whenever you need me,
As your *Spirit* guide!

I AM, Water

For *I Am, Water*,
   The conduit of all things,
To life— I bring.
   I come forth to nourish
The *Divine Seed of Love*
   Within the human soul,
As the *Divine Essence*
   Of thy *Earth* beholds
Her grace to the *Universe*,
   She shall preserve humanity,
Forever more.

I Can Enjoy You

I can enjoy your smile.
I can enjoy your voice.
I can enjoy your tender touch.
I can enjoy your choice of words
you speak, for it makes my *Spirit* meek.

As I humble my strength
To give protection to your soul—
Bold, becomes my nature,
Gentle, becomes my hands,
As I come to understand
the very nature of a woman.
I can enjoy you.

I Got a Thing for You

Ain't misbehaving,
I got a cravin
In my soul,
Truth be told,
I got a thing for you.

I'll be lyin,
If I don't keep tryin,
To get you back,
Now that's a fact
That I got a thing for you.

In the meantime,
In the *Spring Time,*
I'm gonna get you back,
And that's a fact,
Cause I got a thing for you.

I Return to You

In the solitude of silence
I return to you,
The guiding light
That pierces through
The darkness
Of a broken soul.

Prayers lifted
With each breath,
You take in me—
Divinity
Of the human *Spirit,*
Which carries
The flame of love
In the wind.

As I return to you
Whole,
No longer
Fragmented pieces
Of the *Divine*
But that of flesh
That has risen
To the sanctuary
Of the heavens;

Angelic beings,
Who walk upon thy Earth
To share wisdom
Of thy kingdom of heaven
Which resides within
The Earthly heart
Of the human soul.

I Shall Burn Away Thy Sins

Like a moth
Drawn to a flame,
All forgiven souls
Shall know my name.

Under the veil of darkness,
I shall guide you
To the *Divine light,*
As all is forgiven
At the break of light.

I shall burn away thy sins,
As new life begins—
Again and again…

Your *Divine Spirits* shall rise
Higher, beyond the apex
Of thy *Universe,*
As I release thee
From thy *Earthly* curse.

As thy cosmic soul
Balances thy oceans
With the magnitude
Of *Love*, you shall leave
A token of gratitude;
Crystalline fragments—
Sands of modern times.

I Vow

Calibrate me.
Stimulate me.
Excite my energy, now.
Give it to me, now.
Penetrate, now.
Make me say, wow.
Pure ecstasy.
Erotic fantasy.
Make love to me, now.
At your throne, I bow.
I'm your *Queen*.
You're my *King*.
To your soul, I vow.

I'm Delighted to Say, I Love You

Great Goddess of thy Universe,
I return to you— *Broken,*
Like the crystalline particles
That balances thy beloved *Earth;*

The constant thrust of
Human emotions has pierced
Through to my loving soul,
As I escape the inferno
Of your dying love to save humanity
From its self-inflicting insanity.

Hateful slurs…
Wicked emotions…
Aim for my heart's center,
As the mind's arrow dare to enter
My abyss— A near miss
Of thy *Divine* heart.

Hate, you are forbidden
In this sacred place
Where only infinite love
Occupies all time, and space.

As *Divine Spirits* are reborn,
Nourished by your wicked loathing
For all of humanity,
Loving *Spirits* of thy *Earth*
Shall preserve the souls of thee,
And humanity will no longer
Mourn for you—

As evil sin is forever cleansed
From thy Beloved Earth,
The *Divine Universe* is delighted to say,
I love you.

Intensity

Intensity is
The stronger side of me,
When passion flares
To emit loving energy.

For I come
With grace, to erase
Negativity—
As positivity
Balances the polarities
Of all time and space.

Journey of the Soul

Fragmented dimensions of life,
The journey of the soul—
Painted illusions upon
The tapestry of thy Earth,
As she heals humanity
From the pains of strife;

As the *Divine Spirit*
Rebirths thy soul anew,
Into the likeness of
The *Divine-self,*
The *Unadulterated-self,*
The *Inalienable-self,*
The *Sovereign-self,*
The *Human-self,*
The *Giver of Life-self,*
The *Sustainer of Humanity-self;*
Do we dare not open our eyes to see reality?

Awaken your hearts to receive
Your rightful inheritance—
The Natural Essence of Divine Love!

Justice of Love

For *I Am* the storm that brings
the rain, you clap to my thunder,
as my lightening brings *Divine* energy
to your hollow souls.

You dance in pools of blood
as I bring new life to thee—
One by one, you levitate
to my heavens, as *Spirits* take flight,
to deliver souls to thee.

I am the *Keeper of Divine Time,*
who balances *Truth* and *Justice*
of the human soul. Our two worlds,
torn apart— Left behind are bronze
arrows of love.

Your warrior spears were no match for me,
as my dagger sliced through to your souls.

"I've come to be saved," you say, as you
come knocking on heaven's door,
"I've come to be cleansed of my earthly sins."
"Drain me," you say, *"Purify my blood,*
on the eve of this night, when angels
take flight from your heavens."

As they feast upon the flesh of mortal men,
to prepare the ultimate sacrifice for the *Gods*.
Spare their rod, they did not— As they fought
to their death for a *Divine* cause. The *Gods*
shall feast upon the souls of mortal men—

For each earthly sin they commit,
they must admit, or their souls shall be
devoured by the heavenly *Gods*— As demons
return to *Earth*, to prepare for rebirth,
repent your sins to thee—

Cross your heart and hope to die;
Place 2 silver coins across your eyes,
and repeat after me...
Hear ye, old soul of Lucifer,
who come to claim the souls of thee,
call out thy earthly name!

A child of *God* you are not,
decayed flesh that cannot rot,
for you are diseased, inside out.

As immortal as thy earth, I shall
be rebirthed, and will return
to claim the souls of thee.

Evil shall exist no more,
when thy souls arrive at
heaven's door, thou Angels
I shall release.

One by one, they shall come,
to sing praise of glory, to set
your captives free.

Children of thy *Gods'*, whose
bodies rot, lie as hollow shells
upon thy earth.

Corpse maimed and rotted—
Symbolic reflection of thy sins
committed, upon thy earth.

Before me, you stand acquitted.
Right or wrong you must admit,
and ask for forgiveness;

> *Goddess of Justice*
> *Goddess of Peace*
> *Goddess of Love*
> *Goddess of Me*

Forgive me for my sins,
wipe away thy guilt,
cleanse thy earthly soul of filth.

Bond our hearts in love again,
and cleanse thy souls of sin—
under your shadow of love,
I shall walk thy earth.

Under the moon-lite sky,
we shall never say good bye,
as our hearts conjoined as one;

Under the union of the *Sun,*
justice shall reign throughout
thy earthly *Queendom* forever more,
as your *Divine Love* settle all scores.

Lady, Queen Pharaoh

I was once a Queen,
Celebrated and honored by many titles;
Lady, Queen, Pharaoh,
Ruler of the Nubian Crescent;
My temples remain unearthed.

My Dynasty ruled along the fertile *Nile,*
At the heart and soul of the crescent *Earth,*
Where the *Sun* and *Moon* rejoiced
In her radiant smile.

As birds sang sweet melodies,
The nectar of the most fragrant fruit
Sent an intoxicating aroma for miles.

All great men were drawn to me
For my beauty and essence,
I was the *Tamer of Love;*
Creator of spells and potions;
Re-known mystic of all realms;
Ruler of shadow and darkness;
Caster of Divine Light.

My love spells could put the most
ferocious lions to sleep, and have them
laying at my feet like kittens.
Yet I remained hidden in this jungle
after the great quake shook our nations apart.

We were hit by a storm of meteorites,
That poured from the sky like fiery boulders.
There was nowhere to run, so I ran to the
ocean and fell asleep. When I awaken, I was here.
Where ever here is?

Let it Rain

Let it rain,
As I pour out tears,
Out of fear
Of being hurt again.

I don't wanna sin…
I wanna feel
Free, again.

Holding on to the pain
Deep within
My soul,
As revelations unfold;

Life seems surreal,
This pain I feel,
I wanna let go!

I wanna feel
Love again.

Life as One Whole

As the *Divine Mother*
Nourishes the rebirth of her soul,
Her *Divine Creations*
Shall be of great manifestation
Of *all beings*;

One-half of the equal part
Of thy whole,
Who does not favor
One over the other;

Dare she discriminate
When her masculine conjoins
With its feminine,
To protect her *Divine* yoke;

The shell and strength
Of her *Earthly* skin,
Shall be of kin with all
That it preserves— Within.

Likeness of thee, I AM

From the mouth of thy *Sacred Sea,*
You carried fertile seeds of eternal life,
Along thy Nubian-Arabian Nile,
You nourished me—
Bringing all Divine beings back to life;

Sun shined upon my ambient face,
As I rebirthed the human race,
All things are of me—

Universal crystals of thy *Earth,*
Rebirthed into the likeness of the *I Am,*
My fertile ground shall sustain humanity.

Love Conquers All

Love conquers all,
When human trials and tribulations
Rise above it all.

    Rise about hate…
    Rise above anger…
    Rise above pain…

When positive energy erases the stains
Of negative thoughts, energy and emotions.

When *love* is centered in alignment with the *I Am;*
When *love* is centered on solid ground;
When *love* is the first thought that comes to mind;
When *love* is not blind or submissive to hate;
When *love* stimulates the positive flow of *love,*
Love conquers all.

Love is Bond

Blood and hustle
Shall forever bond us.
To infinity.
May the *Great Spirit*
Ground our *essence*
As we absorb the fallacies
Or our modern-day reality;

As *Divine Truth*
Nourishes our beings
To thrive upon thy *Earth,*
May rebirth of its *essence*
Inspire the *"game"* in me.

You did the time, as did I,
As *Divine Time* unwinds
Within—
All is forgiven
For our *cardinal sins*.

Crimes of passion
We shall commit,
For we have paid the penalties
As we evolve the legacy of
Our bloodlines—

We shall no longer suffer
Our father's transgressions—
Which are forgiven, as fate
Settles old scores—
Love and blessings
We shall create,
Forever more.

As *Fire* is to *Air,*
Your *Divine Love*
Shall be everywhere.
As *Water* is to *Earth,*

I shall nourish rebirth.
From the seeds of
Divine Life,
We shall grow—
Through loving music,
I shall flow.

No weapon shall form
Against my *Divine* will,
As my *norm* shall be of my quill.

To society's norm,
I shall not conform
As *Divinity* transforms *Love*
Into the hearts and minds
Of humanity—
As *Divine Truth*
Becomes day to day
Reality.

Loving Divine

Life simply is what it is,
Not what you want it to be.
Human by designed.
Interchangeable
With *Divinity*

Star beings,
Of thy beloved *Earth*—
Manifestation
Of *Loving Energy*.
Rebirthed.

Allow your actions
To be from your heart,
As your words spark
A chemical reaction
From your mind,
To always speak
And show compassion
On behalf of thy *Loving Divine*.

Loving Thoughts

Along my paths in life
I encounter you,
Guiding and inspiring
In all that I do—

Divine Love,
Rooted within my soul,
Unfolds with each loving thought
That comes to mind.

For my eyes are not blind
To thee— The cure for humanity,
Whose soul is lost,
For another one's cause.

But love shall continue
To guide the way,
In all I *do and say,*
In the *Spirit of Divine Love*

Lust

Lust, I welcome you…
Seductress of temptation
Embody me once again
As our essence commits
Cardinal sins—
Twin flames of passion,
We shall part the heavens
Between us.

Be the *fire* to my *air*
As my *waters* comes ashore.
Earth is but a haven to fulfill
Our most lustful desires—
As our elements unite as one,
We shall adorn her, as she ignites
Our beings in *pure ecstasy.*

Manifestation of Divine Life

Someday soon,
We must all meet our *Divine Creator,*
To raise our hand to thee—
To swear in the presence of the *Almighty,*
Our part in the manifestation of hateful energy.
Transmuted from our thoughts, to our minds,
That has blinded our souls to see,
The wicked actions that has plagued thy *Earth,*
And the self-destruction of humanity.

Upon our reincarnation,
We must take a vow to surrender
Our free thoughts to the *Divine Spirit* above,
As she guides our minds to manifest
The *Divine Energy of Love—*
Within our hearts and soul,
As *Divine Life* unfolds within,
To calibrate our thoughts and actions
Before committing a *cardinal sin.*

We must pledge an oath to the *Universe*
Our duty to preserve humanity,
And all of *Earth's* creations,
As she governs the ecosystem of *Divine Life*
And all of its manifestations.

Moment in Time

The gentle caress of my pillow
When I lay down at night,
Soothes my soul
Like the soft glow
Of your morning essence
When my eyes awaken
To your golden light;

Oh' how I yearn to feel
Your warmth
Against my copper skin,
As you invigorate my *Spirit*
To recapture this moment,
Again and again.

Monarch

When the human soul awakens,
Ready to explode,
Surrender to its Spirit,
As Divinity unfolds—
Like the petals of a lotus,
Release its energy,
Spread your wings
Like a butterfly,
And become the monarch
that you were born to be.

Morning Glory

Love is like a flower
that grows in the wild,
that catches your notice
in a distant view, and inspires
your inner child.

As you travel along a narrow path
for a closer glimpse, You discover
a meadow of daises, A bush of
red roses and pink tulips
that makes you heart smile.

And the sweetest aroma of magnolias,
that line the path, and literally
takes your breath away.
Along your adventurous journey,
you decide to rest awhile.

As time passes you by, night falls.
When you awaken, to your discovery
is *Mother Nature,* and her marvelous
wonders, basking in her *Morning Glory.*

My Harvest Delights

Fruitful is thy *Earth*.
Green pastures.
My *harvest delights*.

Nourished by my oceans,
Energized by my *Moon*
At night.

Noon-day *Sun*
Ripen my orchards,
As my seasons come and go.

As I sustain all life,
Enjoy the fruits of my *Earth*.
New seeds, I shall sew.

Natural Delights

Suckle the fibers
of my mango fruit,
drink of my melons,
as my sweet juices
nourishes the soul of you—
My Divine, earthly beings.

As I detox your loins
with my natural delights,
my ripen berries
shall rejuvenate your *Spirits*
like aged wine,
from the *Heavenly Divine,*
Mother Earth.

Natural Identity

Please excuse me,
While I untangle my weave.
While I allow my natural tresses
To flow in the *Universe's* gentle breeze;
While I reclaim my *Natural* identity.
While I reclaim my *Black* identity.
While I reclaim my *African* identity.
While I reclaim my *Native Indian* identity.
While I let go of a *false* identity.

Please excuse me,
While I untangle your weave!

New Life, is a Star Away

Death of the human soul
Opens the heart to unfold
Love— within.
Perished in a realm of sin;
Only to awaken into the light
Of the higher realms above.

Magnificent Universe,
How vast her wonders.
As she guides the human *Spirit*
To ponder, *which way to go?*

Take it slow, along your journey
Called life— For strife
Balances the natural equilibrium
Of the heart,
That never parts
The soul of the *Divine,*
Who entwines
New Life, within
Thy *Earthly Star.*

Our Fathers, Who Art in Heaven

There is nothing more rewarding
Than receiving the inheritance
Of the teachings and guidance
Of our Heavenly Fathers,
During their time of transition
To a higher realm.

This scared time
Of bereavement
Is a moment of
Gratitude,
Forgiveness,
Unconditional Love,
And a *Deeper appreciation*
For *Divine Life.*

For every Pearl of Wisdom
They passed on to us,
We shall bead each stand
As we reflect upon
His trials and tribulations,
And forgiveness
Of our own transgressions
When we chose
A different path in life.

When the *Holy Spirit*
Receives him in the
Universal Divine Realm
Of thy Heavenly Kingdom,
Our Fathers' Spirit
Will continue to guide us,
And protect us,
As we serve as living legacies
Of their truth, wisdom
And devout service
To the Divine creator.

One Soul

I AM, who I have *come to be*,
Evolved essence of my ancestry.
No longer caged in.
No longer forced to sin.
No longer blind to see
The fabrication of a
Disillusioned society.

A victim of our ancestors' past,
I AM NOT!
Centuries' long atrocities
Committed by a survived soul
Possessed by the essence
Of his VERY own linage.

Oh, how *TRUTH* unfolds
Into the fabric of modern times,
As the *Universe* entwines
All energetic beings
To the essence of *love,*
Once again.

As *Earth* is healed
From the atrocities
Committed against her
Very Own Flesh!
We shall evolve as
    One Being
    One Seed
    One Soul

As *Divine Life* unfolds,
We shall thrive together as
One Human Race—
Caretakers of thy beloved
Mother Earth.

Paradise

Just breathe…
As you try to appease the masses,
Who have placed you in caged glasses,
To provide entertainment to a mind
That has become restless
As they themselves are being tested,
As they prove their resilience
In a world that will soon cause them
To fade away into the night.

Ghostly beings of mystical reality,
To become one with the possession
Of artificial energy—
Once enslaved to a master
That wears a crown.
Before their feet, forced to bow down
To lower your head to the ground
As they sit so high and mighty
Upon a throne—

Centuries past,
Lost souls still roam thy *Earth,*
Seeking rebirth,
Having suffered crucifixion
Upon a "Holy Cross."
The *Holy Grail* does foretell truth,
Once held in the hands of thee.
Liberty does not liberate the soul.
If only the eyes could see
A soul in darkness—
Forced to live in a suffocated world
Of misery, should it forsaken a world
Of paradise.

Peace and Hate

Let us sail into the sunset,
You and I,
To wish the essence of hate
Good bye.

Oh, how greed for power
Has caused the human soul
To go insane—
On its quest to control the world,
And to question thy *Holy name*.

I call upon thee,
For *World Peace*.
One who sits atop
Of the *holiest* thrones,
Great Overseer of thy
Earthly souls—

The balancer of all the oceans
That flows through me.
Your heavenly mist
Is the *Divine kiss*
That soothes my tempered soul.

Your *Divine Love*
Sways me to sleep at night—
My *Earthly* oceans
Basks under your *moonlight,*
As the *Galactic Universe*
Calms my fiery soul;

O' *Love,*
How we meet again,
Under your *sunlight.*
Love, you abandoned me
Many *moons* ago,
But my *Divine* escort

Shall guide me back
To your loving heart.

May we be at *peace* and *harmony*
With who we are,
Guardians of thy Earthly Star.
May the reckoning of our past
Be forgiven,
And our union be as bright
As the morning *Sun*
That shines into our hearts
To bond our love,
As *Peace* and *Hate*
Dearly part.

Peace and Love is My Cause

The only cause worth fighting for
Is "Peace and Love" for our
Beloved *Mother Earth*.
As her *Divine Spirit* awakens
To receive *Divine Love*
From the cosmic *Universe* above.

Her *Universal* delights
Cascades reflections of
Her *Delicate Soul*,
Her *Dark Soul*,
Her *Fertile Essence;*

As she rebirths seeds
Of *Divine Love*,
To nourish all realms
Of existence,
Her inner most beauty
Shall radiate from the hearts
Of *all Divine* species.

May we unite in peace,
As loving and compassionate
Human beings.

Perfect Design

O' *Divine Universe,*
I hereby surrender my essence
To your throne,
No longer will I allow my *Spirit*
To roam
Between dimensional realms,
Not guided by the *Great Divine.*

For time and space
Does not exist in her infinite reality,
The perfect design of humanity,
Where peace and love
Co-exists as *One.*

One Divine Spirit
One Divine Body
One Divine Being

Mother Earth's Perfect design.

Playground of Love

Unfamiliar essence
Overshadows me,
As it awaits
To pierce my veil;

Lust dwells
In the realm of the
Innocence—
Where lonely souls
Go to play;

Purity of the heart
Compounds thy flesh,
When darkness
Meets the light;

Plight of romance
Begins with a kiss,
When lust of the *Spirit*
Remiss thy soul—

Upon manifestation
Of fleshy desire,
Temptation
Fuels the passion
Of *Love*

Positive Vibrations

Divine energy
Transmutes
Positive vibrations
From my thoughts,
Expressions of emotions,
Loving synergy—
Resonates all that *I Am*.

Power of the Hour

Power of the Hour,
Come rescue me,
From the hold of negativity,
As *Divinity* rises within my soul.
As new life unfolds within.

Earth, reborn.
Cleansed of sin.
Baptize my soul
In the *power of love.*
Ground my *Spirit* within
Her *soul,* and the
Universal stars above.

Galactic, I reform.
Essence of all life matter,
No longer shattered
Into pieces.
I Am whole.
I Am all things—

Risen from the depths
Of her oceans— Nourished.
Her *love* potion to heal your pain,
As she rebirths humanity
Again and again—
In the essence of *Divine Love.*

Praise of the Divine

Sacrifice of thy heart,
I shall part
The ways of hate—
For I shall no longer
Be embodied
Into the collective energy
You create.

For my love for the *Divine*
Shall reign over thy Earth,
Who shall nourish
The rebirth of thy
Spiritual essence,
Cosmic Spirit of the Divine,
Who shall uplift my song in praise.

Prayer for Love

As the *Season of Love* begin,
May the *Spirit of the Most High*
Cleanse humanity of sin.
As *she* nourishes all life
Within thy *Earthly* womb
To put chaotic energy to rest.

May the synchronicity
Of all around, encourage us
To do our very best,
As we ground our essence
To thy Earthly ground—
No matter the controversy
We shall rebound
In the name of, *Divine Love.*

Protest, in the Name of Love

As I observe the mantras
displayed on banners across
America's picket lines—
Not a one, speaks of
Peace, Love and Unity.

I guess America has become
the land of *"Free Speech by Protest."*
Giving old souls a rightful voice
to be heard again—

As their sins have yet to be cleansed.
As their wounds have yet to be healed.
As they can no longer, *Rest in Peace.*

Now I lay me down to sleep—
The beginning mantra
of an evening prayer,
before one's *Spirit* takes flight
in the midst of chaos and war.

It'll be lucky to find its way back
to its soul, come sunrise.

Misguided souls, yearning to belong
on one-side, or the other.
Humans, herded like cattle,
into the coffers of Big Corps,
'   America Inc.

An international conglomerate
of *Good vs. Evil*,
as the stock-bell tolls—
Place your bets.
But who's betting on love?

I shall give a token to the *Divine*,
I shall hang my banner on the *Picket Line*,

and protest for *Peace* and *Unity*.
In the name of *Love!*

Purposed for a Season

From cradle to grave
All lives shall be saved
My embryonic cells of life,
Purposed for a season—
I've yet to reason
A clear answer to
Humanity's strife.

Why can't life be
As simple as breathing,
Meditating like statues.
Yet we'll be forced
To absorb all the pain
From those who
Weep their anguished cries
At our feet.

There is no escaping
Earth's pain,
To be rebirthed
Again and again—
Recycled once more
To live a thousands
Lives to endure
More pain.

Like her rain,
I pour down
My tears of joy
Unto thy beloved Earth,
Fragmented pieces
Of thy Universe,
I shall put myself
Back together again.

To mend my broken heart
And remold myself
Into a Goddess,

A human replica
Of the Gods!
How's that for
Breaking the cycle
Of life.

The golden inscription
At my feet shall read,
"Wake me when
Humanity has broken
It's curse of sin!"

Ray of Hope

Release me from the chaos
of human sin,
Cleanse away its negative energy
from my *Divine* skin.

Protect me, as you nourish my soul,
within— As new life
of your *Divine Essence* unfolds;

Where eternal darkness dances
in synchronicity with all realms
of your *Divine* light—

As your *Ray of Hope* greets me
At first sight, reflecting rainbows
of cosmic love, below, in-between
and above.

Rebirth of Humanity

Beauty within my soul,
Vast heavens of thy *Universe*
Unfolds *Divine* mysteries within.

Beyond the surface of your skin
Exists all that *I Am,* all that you are,
Divine remnants of thy *Earthly star.*

Star seeds of thy beloved *Earth*,
Fertile essence of thy loins—
Immaculate conception of *Divine* life,
Rebirth of humanity
Is what your heart and souls shall see.

Recycle of thy Soul

Grievance of the heart
Weakens the soul
To surrender
To the collective *Spirit*—
When the flag of compassion
And sympathy is raised
To bring forth unity.

For the concept of unity
Is not to merely unite
In the moments of sorrow,
But as a controlled collective,
To surrender to the desires
Of another— Who mourns death
In celebration of riches.

For only our beloved *Mother Earth*
Can comfort the *Spirit*
During a time of mourning.
Her Divine essence receives
And replenishes all seeds of life.

Reincarnation of Life

Love is,
My *vibration*...
My *sensation*...
My *creation*...
My *revelation*...
Love is my flow of energy.

In synergy, I flow
With the *loving essence*
Of the *Divine Universe*.

With each rhyme, word,
Verb— Stroke of my pen,
I began, again.
Reincarnation of life,
In the *Name of Love*.

Restless Mind, Syndrome

Many thoughts
   Have circled
My mind,
   But I've been
Too distracted
   By one thought
Over the other,
   To clearly see
Which thought
   Was more important
Than the other,
   But it would require
More thought
   Just to sort out
The existing thoughts…
   More thinking…
More thoughts…
   More thinking…
The mind can't rest
   Before another thought
Enters a restless mind.

Return of Eden

I hear your thunder roar,
From the agony of chaos;
Deeply embedded within
The human soul.

It shall exist no more,
As the *Power of Love*
Comes ashore—
Risen from the depths
Of the mighty seas,
To heal humanity.

Rebirthed souls,
Cleansed of *Earthly* sins
To restore *love*
Once again.

Return of Eden—
The way *Mother Earth*
was meant to be.

Reunion

I awoke to your glory,
Thine morning sunrise,
Greeting me with the brightest
Golden Smile I'd ever seen.

It's been days of downpour
And cabin fever
Has gotten the best of me,
As I grow more contempt
Of this smoggy weather
In Georgia's most unusual
Winter season.

Just last week,
We brought in the New Year,
And tomorrow's temps
Will be sixty-five degrees.
O' *Morning Glory,*
I wish you could
Stay for a while.

Never before have I seen
Georgia's bedrock
Torn apart, to the ore
Of her soul,
As her soaked Earth
Compounds her
Bloodstained clay.

I'm sure after the
Fracking and quaking
Is complete, and new housing

And commercial business
Developments get underway,
Her wandering Spirits
Will find a new resting place,
As they aimlessly roam
Upon our earthly plain.

For her atmosphere
Is not the same,
And so many dimensional portals
Have become gateways
For souls, to gather in union
Wherever they want.
May they pass on
Loving blessing,
As they cross through
One life, to the next.

Right Hand of God

Do I need to *Slap You*
With the *Right hand of GOD*,
As she draws her rod
To show you who's boss?

The countless corpse
That lay to rot—
Vaulted within thy earth,
Came at a hefty cost.

Yet I prefer to receive
The *Spirit* in the *Wind*,
To sustain the soul of humanity
When new life begins, again.

All this war and chaos
Is nearly driving me insane,
As the collective masses
Becomes more disdain
Over who's right
Or who's wrong,
As the weary cries for *Freedom*
Continues on.

A soul unevolved
Becomes a desolate soul,
Left to wander upon thy Earth,
To be devoured by predators
Who prey on the weakness
Of the human mind—

Which forces my intervention,
So I shall reserve the slap

Until another time,
And entwine your hearts and soul
With the *Power of Love,*
So be thankful to the *Universe* above
Who can never Rest in Peace,
For the sake of preserving humanity.

Righteousness

The conscience of the *soul,*
is the *Universal* conscience
of the *heart.*

Universal eyes
within the inner being
of the conscience *mind.*

Dimensional thoughts
between realms
of all existence.

Righteousness,
The path of freedom.

Righteousness,
The path of liberation.

Righteousness,
The path of love.

Righteousness,
The path to healing
humanity.

Season of Love

May the *Season of Love*
Now begin, as humanity
Is cleansed of its sins.
As a new season of
Peace, Love and Joy,
Fill our souls
Within in;

We shall,
Embrace it…
Magnify it…
Praise it…
Reflect it…
Glorify it…
Receive it…
Perfect it…
And evolve
Into a more *loving,*
And *peaceful*
Human race.

Secrets of the Soul

There is no need to conceal
The secrets of my mystery,
As dark ages passes you by.
My shadow essence
Shall remain, to sing to you
Sweet lullabies, to soothe
Your tempered soul.

As you seek my guiding light
In your dreams,
As my *Spirit* carries your *soul*
In the wind,
I shall return it to thy flesh
At day break.

Life is not what it seems,
As your *soul* is tested
With each word you speak.
Even the energy you emit
From your body language
Down to the company you keep.

In the perils of modern-day,
When *War* seems to be
More of a priority
Than *Love*.
The average soul lives a lonely
And miserable life, as strife
Compounds the soul
Of thy *Beloved Earth*.

As the advances of technology
Continues to exceed
The average intelligence
Of society's collective minds,
Who are being controlled
By remote sensors that hover above,
And has breached the boundaries

Of the Divine Universe,
Help is on its way! So stay
Pray Up!

One day the curse will be broken
And your Spirits will be set Free!
I shall continue to guide your essence
To the *Flame of Hope*.
Oh' how the pleasantries
Of those very words
Soothes my tempered soul—
To know that I'm thought of,
Always.

Self-Love

Reinvent yourself.
Search deep within
To connect with your
Divine Self—
To become the best
Replica of You!

Shine,
In your own
Divine Light!
There is nothing
More magical than
Self-Love.

Serenity and Bliss

Oh' sweet oceans,
How I miss
Your gentle waves.
Your stillness.
Your calmness.

Thoughts of you
Brings back better days,
Of love and peace,
That's in the air.

As your majestic waves
Comes ashore,
To spread *Divine Love*
Everywhere.

Oh' *Sunlight Glory,*
Shine down on me.
As your majestic story
Shall be told
To infinity—

Of how your *Divine Rays*
Captures every movement
Of thy oceans,
As her potion becomes
The antidote to heal
The human soul.

As we create better days,
More peaceful and loving days.
As your way, becomes our way,
To guide our souls to your
Divine loving light.

Sing to Me

Your voice
soothes the pain
in my somber soul,
Like the soft melody
of wind chimes,
that carries harmonic
vibrations in the wind.

Sing to me,
Your gentle words…

Sing to me,
I love you…

Sing to me,
Sweet lullabies…

To soothe my
broken heart,
and comfort
my pain.

Sing to me.

Skin

There is a strong division of *culture*
That our eyes can see,
Such division has existed
Throughout antiquity.

Barbarism, has since arisen,
Suppressed since the
Beginning of time.
Buried deep within
Mother Earth's core,
By the *Great Divine*.

Fragmented pieces of herself;
Her *Ethereal-self,*
Her *Resurrected-self,*
Her *Divine-self,*
Her one-half of a *Divine Whole*-self—
Cosmic fragments of galaxies unknown.

Crystalline fragments of etheric
Energy roam throughout the *Universe,*
As *Earth* and other planets becomes
A new haven to call home.

Craving to be united once again,
Cultures, divided by the entity
We call skin.

Barbarism has arisen!
A dark reminder
Of our ancestors sins!
Do we dare live the aftermath
Again?

Soul Creation

As my soul is set free
From the wickedness of hate,
The *Universe* reminds me
Of the beautiful world
She creates.

Love is her essence,
As she opened my eyes to see
The reality of an angry man's soul,
Who seeks to capture the *Spirit*
Of the *whole*— *Divine* essence in me.

Bodies, falsely imprisoned
By make believe fantasies of a *savior*,
Said, to represent *Divinity*.

Great Teachers of the Ages,
Devout Sages, passes on her teachings
From generation to the next,
As we scribe the text
Of her Divine wisdom,
To nourish the souls of her
Earthly children.

In our hearts and minds
Lies the seeds
Of her soul creation—
Divination.

Soul-Purpose

*What will soon destroy the faith of humankind,
but that of our own minds…*

We live in a modern-day society,
Where *Beliefs* opposes *Beliefs,*
Over what to *believe*—
As old beliefs are challenged
With *New Thoughts, Ideas,*
And *Free-Spirited* behavior,
From evolved minds
That no longer believes
That the *Savior*
Of the human soul
Are ancient tales, once told
To control the minds
Of the masses.

As groups are placed in
Economic classes, to become
Demographics that serves
A corporate entity,
Designed to control the free-will
Of humanity,
Who will be forced to go underground
To simply breathe—
To be set free
From those above,
Who opposes unity and love,
And work in concert to cultivate
A replica of what Earth naturally rebirths.

Hybrids of artificial life,
Once ingested, immediately
Goes into strife, with the biosphere
Within the human flesh,
To evolve into a discombobulated,
Restless *Spirit*—
One can't rest a mind

That blinds itself to the needs
Of the body, but feeds
Into the *Spirit* of another man's ego.
Humanity must learn to let go
Of beliefs— *Fallacies,*
And awaken to the reality
Of humanity's soul-purpose
And be at peace with the soul
Of the *Great Spirit*, that connects all life
To the soul of the *Divine Universe*.

Sparrows in the Sky

Playful sparrows in the sky,
I watch, as the joy life
passes me by.

Their delicate wings
Carried by the wind,
In flight with the loving energy
Of *Mother Earth*.

Their *Spirits,* in unison
With her harmonic
Vibrations.

Not a care in the world
As their *Spirit* soar,
Their joyful nature
Is simply to be adored.

Spirit of Love

Let not the opportunity
To embrace peace and love
Pass us by.
But allow the virtue
And essence of their wisdom
Be reflected from our *Divine Hearts*.

The misdeeds of yesterday
Are already forgiven
Unless you chose to repeat
The mistakes of your past.

At last, *the Spirit of Love*
Awakens us at sunrise—
At the first break
Of the first morning light,
As our collective Spirit
Bask in the *Glory*
Of the *Divine Universe*.

Spirit of Peace

As I seek refuge
Beneath your
Angelic wings,
I shall rejoice in
The *Spirit of Peace*,
Your protection brings.

May *Divine Love*
Be restored upon
Thy *Earth* —
Within the *Spirits,*
Minds and *Souls*
Of humanity—
As we restore
Our connection
To *source* energy.

Spirituality

Take refuge in my *Orb*.
The Universe created you.
Protected from the social norms
Of the world,
Which seek to devour you.

There is nothing artificial about me,
You will realize it
When you reach the realm
Of *Divinity*.

As above,
So below,
In-between—
Is all of me.

To explore the depths
Of my essence
Is to believe in,
Spirituality.

Star Wisdom

Poetry, is mere
Flow of energy
That resonates
From deep within
My soul,
As tales of life
Between
Dimensional realms
Unfolds,
Truth.

Divine Truth,
Shine your
Star Wisdom
Upon thee,
Through the craft
Of poetry,
As I nourish
The soul
Of humanity
With the essence
Of your *Divine*
Loving Energy.

Straighten Up and Fly Right

Straighten up and fly right,
Was the last words she said to me...

When I left my old life
And went farther South
To explore life
To see what's it's all about,
I traveled the world
And crossed the *Seven Seas,*
All I have left are the words
She said to me—
As she guides my steps
And watch over me,
I will always fly along the path
That she have set for me.

Sustainability of Humanity

I've learned through my short time
on *Mother Earth,* that the only way
we can save humanity from self-destruction,
is to start by showing more appreciation
for *Mother Earth*, and her vast resources.
Not for the benefit of advancing greed,
power and control over others,
but for its richness, abundance,
and overall sustainability of humanity.
If we destroy it all, her *natural vegetation…*
What will we have left?

Sweet Potato Pie

Greedy chile,
Greedy chile,
Come sit here at my table
And eat a while.
Kick off ya shoes,
Relax those jeans,
Let me show you how
Momma Nean
Throw down on some
Collard greens,
Cornbread,
Potato salad,
Mac and cheese,
And fried chicken,
That's so finger-licken good,
It'll make you wanna
Thank your moma
For teaching you
How to appreciate
Some good old fashion
Southern comfort food,
That's not only good
For your soul
But reminds you
Of the days of old,
When your feet
Were never tired
In the kitchen,
When it came to the fixins,
And don't forget to
Save room for a slice
Of *sweet potato pie!*

Take Me There

Lustful temptations
Seduces my mind
When I think of you;
Erotic foreplay
Of sensual emotions
Excites my loins,
Stimulates my senses—
I'm hypnotized;

By the thoughts of your
Poetic verses, as I drift
Into the galactic realm
Of ecstasy,
From the sound of your
Baritone voice, as you
Envelope my soul's center,
With your sensual
Harmonic melodies.
My senses beckons you
To embrace all of me
With your spoken words.

Take me there,
Beyond the stars!
As I set flight this starry night.

Take me there,
Beyond the Black Heavens!
As the ecstasy of love
Becomes my new haven

Take me there,
Fulfill my most erotic desires!
As our souls conjoin as *One.*

Take me there...
In the name of *Divine Love!*

The Aftermath

There is a strong division of *human culture*
That our eyes can see— Such, division
Has long existed, throughout antiquity.

Barbarism, has since arisen,
Suppressed since
The beginning of time—
Buried deep within
Mother Earth's core
By the *Great Divine*;

Fragmented pieces of *herself,*
Her *Ethereal-self,*
Her *Evil-self,*
Her *Resurrected-self,*
Her *Divine-self,*
Her *One-half* of a
Divine Whole, self.

Cosmic fragments
Of galaxies unknown,
Throughout the *Universe,*
Crystalline fragments roam;

Earth and other planets
It's new haven– Craving
To be united once again;

Cultures, divided
By the entity we call skin,
Barbarism, serves as
An evil reminder of
Our ancestors sins.

Do we dare live out the aftermath,
Once again?

The Evolution of Humanity

As a new day ascends,
Let us be thankful for
Yesterday,
And what tomorrow brings—
A stronger connection to
The *Divine Universe,*
And her vast wonders,

As she allows us to soar
To new heights,
Beyond human will,
As we champion
The evolution of humanity,
Through the essence of
Our *freewill.*

The Sound of Love

The energy of love
Emits from my soul—
The depths of my abode.
Traveled through
Multi-dimensions
Of time and space.

Arriving to a place of
Peace and solitude—
Sensations of thy heart
Remains still,
As my harmonic *being*
Pulsates
The energy of *Love*.

Each beat,
Each pulse,
Each vibration,
Carries the sound
Of the *Universe*—
In harmony
With the
Sound of Love.

Token Seeds of Love

Your copper glow,
Reflects from the silver
Within thy *Earth;*
Her golden peaks,
Green leaf valleys,
Crystalline oceans
Of rebirth;

Elements from
Thy *Universe,*
Fragmenting within
Thy *Earth*—
Planets, orbiting,
Within thy space,
Desiring to take
Your place;

Fertile ground,
I give root—
Infused by the
Moon above;
As thy *Earth* nourishes
Seeds of eternal life,
May infinite *Love*
Be rife.

True Love

Key historical events
are destined
to repeat itself,
if we lend our faith
to its demise—
Negative thoughts,
transformed into reality,
as hate fills
our veil-covered eyes.

Do we not see
that *Love* awaits us,
to simply open
our hearts to receive?
As long as we believe
in the *Divine Power of Love*,
to awaken our eyes
to preserve humanity.

We must lift the wicked
veil of hate, to celebrate
once again, the coming of our
Almighty Savior—*True Love,*
as we, ourselves, rid
our thoughts and hearts
of sin.

Unconditional Loving Energy

Heavenly Universe,
As you blanket thy *Earth*
With your essence,
May your *Divine Spirit*
Embody my soul.

Nourish my core
With unconditional love,
Infuse my sacred abode.

I surrender my *will*
To your grace,
As old habits are erased—
Cleanse humanity of its
Darkest sins, as the
Season of Love begins.

Unleash My Soul

Little lonely lost child,
Soul stuck in the wild,
Where did your *Spirit* go?

Nowhere to *Run*…
Just follow the *Sun,*
Down to the *Riverbend.*

There, you will find
A man who is blind,
He will tell you
Which way it flows.

Union of the Heart

Do not fear *love*.
Embrace it.
As *love* embraces you.

Do not fear *compassion*.
Embrace it.
As *compassion* embraces you.

Do not fear *peace*.
Embrace it.
As *peace* embraces you.

Do not fear *unity*.
Embrace it.
As *unity* embraces you.

Love,
Compassion,
Peace,
Unity,
The perfect union.

Unite as One Human Race

My first message of the *New Year*,
May it greet you with *Divine Love*
And *Good Cheer*—

For the past is now behind us,
As we will no longer fuss
Over who's *most superior*
To be the caretakers
Of our beloved *Mother Earth*.

History has proven itself!

As *Mother Earth* receives
Devout protection
From the *Divine Universe*—

Collectively, we shall mend
Her broken heart,
Not even the energy of *Hate*
Can tear us apart—

As we *Unite* as *ONE*
Human Race.

For in her *Heavenly Dimensions*
She has no place
But for only *Love!*

Unity, is Not Divided

When you attempt to censor
Every word I say,
You ignite the passion within my soul
To thrive— Unity and Compassion
Keeps humanity alive.

Words spoken,
Becomes a token of goodwill.
As I lend to its *Divine Essence*
With the artisan of my quill.

When you attempt to rob me
Of my *Spiritual* worth,
You awaken the core of the *Earth*.
Her love for humanity
Gives her a reason to live.

As she delivers us from the pit of hell,
Where ancient souls forever dwells;
Our vessels guides the way
To deliver them from the rapture of
Love vs. Hate. Collectively,
We become the force of the
Energy we create.

Universal Design

As the veil of darkness
Protects my soul at night,
From acts of immortal sin,
New life arises within my soul,
Each day, it repeats itself again.

Demons roar, as they soar,
Between dimensions of immortal time.
The heart's refuge from itself,
Is governed by the laws
Of the *Universal Divine*.

Universal Harmony

Flow as one, with my
Universal harmony.
Give of your freewill,
For just one dance with me.

Dance in my essence,
To the natural rhythm
That you were born to be—
An instrument upon my Earth.
A conduit for my *Divine Universe.*

As my cosmic planets
Align themselves
With my beloved Earth,
I shall energize your souls
With the *Spirit of Love,*

As she reciprocates her love
To the *Divine Universe* above,
To all beings below,
We shall bestow
Peace, Love and Harmony.

Universal Love, Reborn

As you nourish my soul,
I receive *goodness*
Of your *Divine Will,*
As my *Free Will*
Surrenders to your love.

As Above,
So below,
We bestow,
Universal Love.

Universe, I AM,
Conversations with the Universe

When the *Universe* woke up,
And decided to sing,
Who knew what wonders
She would bring.
When her thunder roars,
And her vibration claps,
Even the holiest of scriptures
Warned us, not to awaken her
From her nap.

Each mantel of her
Magnificent *Earth* shifts,
When her resonance sets adrift
In the wind— Compounding
More layers to her *sands of time*—
As her *Soulful Essence* unwinds.

Oh how her crystal-gems
Sparkles under her *moonlight*,
As the majesty of her auras
Shines bright— Upon sunrise,
Her brightest *Star* nourishes
The most desolate beings
Upon of her worn skin—
Camouflaged to blend
Into the dry desert wind.

Each life form has a story to tell.
How it once dwelled— Thriving
Upon her fruitful *Earth*.

"Do not age my beauty," she says,
For *I AM*, a *Sage,* of all times.
Should I recede my *waters,*
And flood the gates of your heaven;
I shall rejuvenate the tiniest fiber
of my being.

In the meantime, I rejoice in
What *I AM* seeing…
Humanity, destroy itself.

Universe, I Give Thanks to Thee

Universe,
I give thanks to you.
For nourishing my soul
With the essence of you.

Thanks, for the *air*
That I breathe—
My sustainer of
Divine life.

Thanks, for the elements
Which compounds
Thy *Earth*— For the *fire*
Which fuels the passion
Of my *Divine soul*.

Thanks, for your *waters*
Which nourishes
My *Divine Spirit*.

I AM all things,
Thanks to you!
Divine Universe.

Verses of Creation

When *Divinity*
Claims your heart,
You must part
The ways of hate—
For *love* is the energy
The *Universe* creates.

To sin,
Is to begin again,
When lessons learned
Becomes the
Healing mantra
For the *Spirit,*
Mind, Body
And *Soul*—

As the evolution of life
Unfolds, to *New thoughts,*
Ideas, and *Verses of creation*—
To bring about the
Manifestation of the true
Advancement of humanity,
(not technology)
Before it reaches
The brink of insanity;

To recondition the
Human *Spirit,*
Is to never give up
On its *Universal* soul,
Lost, for a good cause—
A heart that seeks Unity,
Compassion, Love and Peace,
Within.

We Shall Never Part

To you, *I Am,* Love.
To you, *I Am,* Energy.
To you, *I Am,* All things,
That you were born to be.

As *love* co-exists within our hearts—
Conjoined in the *Name of Love,*
We shall never part.

Love is the strength of all things,
Created in the *Name of Love.*
There is no stronger bond
With the *Universe.*

We, The People

We, the People, whose voices
Grow stronger by the day,
Let's not ignore the voices
Of the children, as their souls
Become easy prey.

Preyed upon by the wicked ones
Who sit atop their evil thrones,
Whose *Spirits* possess a realm
That has become a haven
For the wicked to freely roam.

We, the People, shall thrive
In unity, as our *love* for humanity
Nourishes the souls of thee—
As compassion within our hearts
Conjoin in the *Name of Love,*
As a new generation is seeded
And nourished by the *almighty* above.

Together we shall forge a new destiny,
Bonded in the name of *liberty*—
For each and every one of us
Was born free— Freedom of the
Spirit, Mind, Body and Soul
Shall release us from curses of old.

Tomorrow we shall live as one,
As we thrive in solidarity
Under the goodness
Of the *Almighty Sun.*

Who Are You?

Who are you?
Where did you come from?

Born within my womb.
Seeded upon my *Earth*.
Nourished upon your birth.
It is my air that you breathe.
It is upon my earth that you bleed.

You walk upon *my Earth*.
Since your birth,
I have nourished you.
There is no valley that you must walk.
There is no hill that you must climb.
Be still my child— *Be still.*

I shall nourish you
With my *Air*,
With my Fire,
With my *Water*,
With my *Earth*.

You are the *Air*.
You are the *Water*.
You are the *Fire*.
You are the *Earth*.

You are all things,
And all things are of you.

As my *Spirit* guides you
To live a fruitful life,
I shall teach you
The essence of me—
The essence of all things.

Divine Seeds upon my *Earth*,
That is who you are.

My *earthly* stars.
Look up in the sky
And say goodbye.
Look down below
And say hello,
To my *Universe*.

For it is the painting
I draw for you,
To encourage you
To be the stars upon my *Earth*.

I gave birth to you
To be the deliverer of thee *All,*
The hope for the future—
The Divine part of me.

Be part of me, my child.
My *Universe*.
My seeds.
I Love You!

Wild-Spirit

Dare you try to tame
A *Spirit* of the wild;
I was set free as a child,
To explore the canvas
Of thy *Universe' Earth*—

Rebirthed on the planet
I now call home.
A paradise for
Intimate *Spirits* to roam;
Drawn to the ether light of love—

Connecting all realms *below*
With dimensions *above;*
In-between we shall be,
Ethereal masses of loving energy.

X-Factor of Love

Don't cancel me out
Without considering
The essential needs
Of the heart.

We live in a realm
So filled with hate,
That with each breath
We take, we create
A replica of a demonic force
That is not a derivative
Of its original source.

Shall we rewind (shift)
The sands of time,
Back to the *true source*
Of our reality—
Whose mission
Was to create *"Quality"*
Divine beings;

To evolve thy *Earth*,
As she inherits her place
In the galactic order
Of the *Divine Universe*.

Again, Don't cancel me out,
Until you know,
Without a doubt,
That *love* conquers all.

Yin-Yang, One

As my feminine and masculine
Essence, conjoin within my
Universal soul— To become *One,*
Fertile Crescent of my *Moon*
Conjoin within the whole
Of the *Sun.*

As *Earth* stands between us,
To be the center of our hearts,
May her *Divine Spirit* embody us,
To forever seal our loving hearts.

Your Will, Shall Be Done

As I prepare to lay my head down to rest,
I surrender my will to the almighty *Universe*.
For I have done my best.

Scribing the sins of humanity
Has not been easy,
There is so much negativity,
Yet so much more left to see.

Being a shield of the human heart
Has taught me that we shall never part.
May you strengthen me with the *Power of Love*,
From below and above—

As my Divine Essence helps to balance
All things in-between, as we become
More enlightened and loving human beings.

Your glory shall be done
Upon the rise of the morning *Sun,*
As I give praise to our *Mother Moon,*
Our hearts shall conjoin each day at noon.

Your will, shall be done!
Your will, shall be done!
Your will, shall be done!

Zen

Zen, is your essence,
Flow through me,
With the *loving Spirit*
Of poetry.

With each rhyme,
And rhythm—
Truism speaks from
Within my soul.

Bold, are my words
Of choice— As your
Spiritual essence
Nourishes my voice.

Moist, are your oceans
That gives new life to me,
As I become whole
With *Divinity;*

To resonate the beauty,
Enlightenment,
And soulful embodiment
Of poetry.

Zero Gravity

We live in a time of zero gravity,
As the *essence of hate* sinks us
Into the abyss of our daily reality.

Waring forces amongst forces,
Who seek to unwind time,
Simply to capture our minds
To become blinded by the fallacies
Of political uproar.

Conditioned minds
Seeking to settle old scores,
When the fact that greed,
The strongest force of them all,
Is being socially ignored.

As empires rise and fall,
None will stand as tall as
The heavenly stars;

Who will continue to shine on
The hearts of humanity, before
We reach the brink of insanity,
As we are guided back to our heart's
Center, as a reminder, that there is still
Hope for us yet.

As fallacies are being understood,
Learn to let GO, if it does not serve
Your highest GOOD!

One Heart…
One Soul…
One Earth…

www.ingramcontent.com/pod-product-compliance
Lightning Source LLC
Chambersburg PA
CBHW070552160426
43199CB00014B/2479